Read for a Better World™

TRANSPORTATION

A Look at THEN and NOW

PERCY LEED

GRL Consultant, Diane Craig, Certified Literacy Specialist

Lerner Publications ◆ Minneapolis

Educator Toolbox

Reading books is a great way for kids to express what they're interested in. Before reading this title, ask the reader these questions:

What do you think this book is about? Look at the cover for clues.

What do you already know about transportation in the past?

What do you want to learn about transportation in the past?

Let's Read Together

Encourage the reader to use the pictures to understand the text.

Point out when the reader successfully sounds out a word.

Praise the reader for recognizing sight words such as *to* and *in*.

TABLE OF CONTENTS

Transportation Then and Now

People have always needed to get from place to place.

THEN

People moved with wagons.

Have you ever moved?

NOW

People move with trucks.

THEN

Horses pulled people around.

NOW

People ride in cars.

THEN

Ships took people to new lands.

NOW

People ride ships to have fun.

THEN

Cities had trolleys.

NOW

Cities have trains and buses.

THEN

The first car was built.

NOW

Cars come in many colors and sizes.

THEN

Planes began to fly.

Have you ever been in a plane?

NOW

Planes fly very high and far.

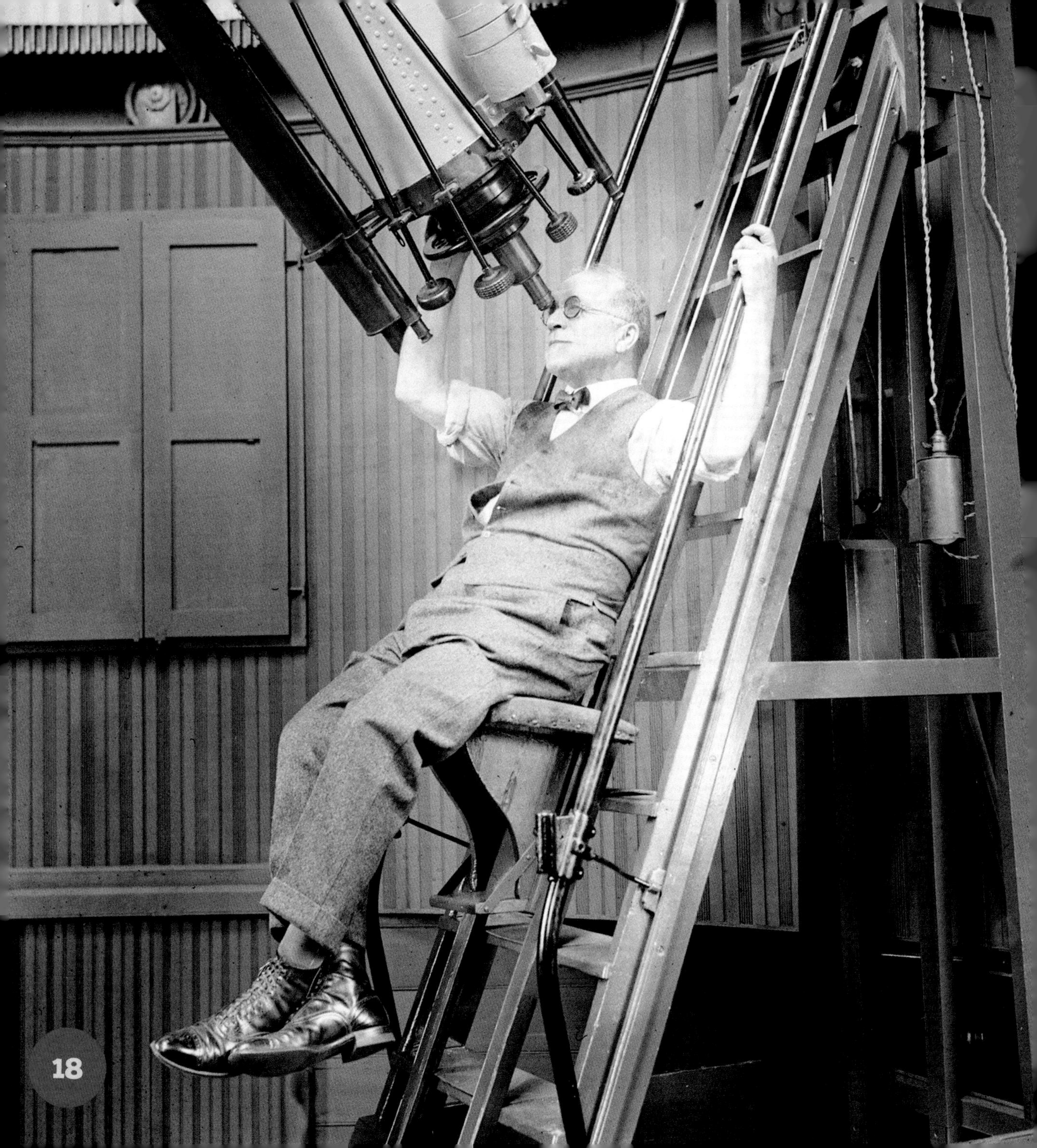

THEN

People dreamed of going to outer space.

NOW

Spaceships take us there.

Would you want to go to space?

There are many new ways to get from place to place.

You Connect!

How do you get from place to place?

How would your life be different without cars?

How can you learn more about how people got around in the past?

Social and Emotional Snapshot

Student voice is crucial to building reader confidence. Ask the reader:

What is your favorite part of this book?

What is something you learned from this book?

Did this book remind you of any ways you get around?

Opportunities for social and emotional learning are everywhere. How can you connect the topic of this book to the SEL competencies below?

Relationship Skills
Self-Awareness
Social Awareness

Photo Glossary

spaceship

train

trolley

wagon

Learn More

Dinmont, Kerry. *Transportation Past and Present*. Minneapolis: Lerner Publications, 2019.

Koestler-Grack, Rachel A. *Airplanes from Then to Now*. Mankato, MN: Amicus Ink, 2021.

Lawrence, Carol. *Transportation: From Then to Now*. Chicago: Albert Whitman & Company, 2021.

Index

Photo Acknowledgments

The images in this book are used with the permission of: © FatCamera/iStockphoto, pp. 4–5; © Wikimedia Commons, pp. 6, 10, 14–15, 23 (wagon); © kali9/iStockphoto, p. 7; © Everett Collection/Shutterstock Images, pp. 8, 12, 18, 23; © kate_sept2004/iStockphoto, p. 9; © NAN104/iStockphoto, p. 11; © YinYang/iStockphoto, pp. 13, 23 (train); © Bim/iStockphoto, p. 15; © Library of Congress, p. 16; © Elenathewise/iStockphoto, p. 17; © Tony Gray and Tim Powers/NASA, pp. 19, 23 (spaceship); © Kiwis/iStockphoto, p. 20.

Cover Photographs: © aapsky/iStockphoto (train); © bauhaus1000/iStockphoto (inset)

Design Elements: Mighty Media, Inc.

Lerner Publications Company
An imprint of Lerner Publishing Group, Inc.
241 First Avenue North
Minneapolis, MN 55401 USA

For reading levels and more information, look up this title at www.lernerbooks.com.

Main body text set in Mikado a Medium.
Typeface provided by Hannes von Doehren.

Library of Congress Cataloging-in-Publication Data

Names: Leed, Percy, 1968–author.
Title: Transportation : a look at then and now / Percy Leed.
Description: Minneapolis : Lerner Publications, [2024] | Series: Read about the past (Read for a better world) | Includes bibliographical references and index. | Audience: Ages 5–8 | Audience: Grades K–1 | Summary: “From trolleys and wagons to cars and spaceships, transportation has changed over the years. Descriptive text and historical photographs give readers a peek into the ways we used to get around”– Provided by publisher.
Identifiers: LCCN 2022037149 (print) | LCCN 2022037150 (ebook) | ISBN 9781728491509 (library binding) | ISBN 9798765603567 (paperback) | ISBN 9781728499581 (ebook)
Subjects: LCSH: Transportation–History–Juvenile literature.
Classification: LCC HE152 .L44 2023 (print) | LCC HE152 (ebook) | DDC 388–dc23/eng/20220825

LC record available at https://lccn.loc.gov/2022037149
LC ebook record available at https://lccn.loc.gov/2022037150

Manufactured in the United States of America
1 - CG - 7/15/23